FROM

GOOD

TO

GREAT

A PRACTICAL AND SPIRITUAL GUIDE TO ENCOURAGE ALL WALKS OF LIFE TO SHIFT FROM A PLACE OF COMPLACENCY TO YOUR GREATEST POTENTIAL

T. Nicole, MBA

ISBN 978-1-64471-891-9 (Paperback)
ISBN 978-1-64471-892-6 (Digital)

Covenant Books, Inc.
11661 Hwy 707
Murrells Inlet, SC 29576
www.covenantbooks.com

This book is dedicated to my Pastor and First Lady, Superintendent Lovelle Butler and Lady April Butler and My Parents, Ben and Charlene Jimison. Thank you for serving as a daily inspiration. I am because You Are!

CONTENTS

PREFACE

It was once stated by an anonymous writer that we are not judged by what we started but rather by what we are able to finish. In other words, it is not in what we begin that carries the most value, but rather it is in what we complete that holds the most significance.

We are now living in a day and time where we have become gung ho about starting trends but have become relaxed and lackadaisical when it comes to executing strategies. We've become quick to begin something but deterred when it comes to completing what we've started. Everyone under the sound of my voice has been given a God-given assignment before the foundations of the world in an effort to increase the body of Christ. And a lot of times as believers when pursing our assignment, once faced with many of life's obstacles and challenges, we tend to lose that same motivation prior to taking on what God has called us to do.

Many of us can testify that when God first called us to our divine place in him, there was a certain excitement that we had but somewhere in the middle of life's adversities and disappointments. We've somehow lost that same vitality that we once portrayed. We've lost that same eagerness that we've once had.

I can recall the times when I was younger and I was preparing for the first day of school. Like most, I was excited about the new school year to see my friends and show off my new clothes and shoes but as the time progressed and that excitement wore off and the responsibility of what was expected of me in the school year started to kick in, the more I lost my enthusiasm. And I can tell you that this is what's taking place within the body of Christ. We are getting excited over what God starts in us but shy away from the expectations of what he's called us to do. We'll accept the calling but neglect the accountability that comes with it. And I can tell you that this is why we got so many people quitting on their God-given assignments. Preachers have stopped preaching. Worshippers have stopped worshiping. Prayer warriors have stopped praying all because we have the tendency to get so enthralled over the emotionalism of what God has assigned us to do but then negate the responsibility that's associated with what he's assigned.

The problem with some of us, we don't like to be developed because development takes time. It takes work. It takes diligence. It takes accountability. And because of this, a lot of times, we have a habit of quitting in the middle of the process and we don't get fully developed. And I can tell you that anything that is not fully developed cannot possibly operate at its fullest potential.

Some of us wonder why we're stuck in certain phases in our lives, why we can't seem to progress in certain areas. I can tell you why. It's because there's still some development that needs to take place. That's why we have to allow God to continue to build us simply because we cannot possibly complete what God has given to us with our zeal alone because when the enemy comes and attacks the assignment of God on our lives, we're going to need more zeal to sustain us. You are going to need more excitement to keep you, but you are going to need some power to keep you from quitting when it seems as if your purpose is stagnant. You are going to need some grace to keep you from walking away when nobody is seemingly supporting your vision. You are going to need some inner encouragement to keep you going when it seems as if you're all by yourself. You are going to need some substance because substance is my proof of what God can do.

Substance reminds me of the power of God. It tells me that if God did it for me, then he can do it for me now. If he delivered me, then he can deliver me now!

Chapter 1

Do You Know Who You Are?

For many are called, but few are chosen.
—Matthew 22:14

When we look at the word *chosen*, it stems from the Greek word eklektos[1] in which simply means "to be handpicked or to be elected." This suggests to me that when you're chosen by God, you are selected to complete a certain assignment that's within the kingdom of God. John 15:16 even declares to us that we didn't choose ourselves, but rather God has chosen us and appointed us to bring forth fruit.

This now simply suggests to me that the choosing of God is not depicted upon our financial status, it's not determined by our capabilities or skills but rather by the purpose that God has embedded on the inside of us. This further lets me know that you and I were chosen on purpose.

Can I help you when I tell you that the choosing of God is not just by happening but rather predestined even before the worlds were created?

---

[1] https://biblehub.com/greek/eklektoi_1588.htm.

The Bible proves this theory when it was pronounced in Jeremiah chapter 1 verse 5 that before we were formed in our mother's womb, God knew us and ordained us. It even goes on to tell us that he called us by name in which signifies familiarity with his creation. This simply means that God looked and pasted our hang-ups and issues and chose to use in spite of.

Even David was a murderer and an adulterer, he still called him a man after his own heart. This suggests to me that our proclivities does not disqualify us from God's choosing, but instead he uses our hang-ups and issues as a way of making us as an eligible candidate for the calling of God that's upon our lives.

Ephesians 4:1 tells us that God chose us even before the foundations of the world. This simply suggest to me that my validation does not come from man, it does not come from a title; but the fact that God has handpicked me out for his glory solidifies my validation and further lets me know that despite what others may think or say, despite what they think or know about you, despite what they may have heard because you and I have been selected by the most high, this indicates that you are anointed, appointed, and approved for a time such as this.

This text now tells us that many are called but few are chosen. As I began to contemplate upon this statement, I became a tad bit curious, and I then began to ask God, "What is necessarily deemed as your chosen?" And he then began to clarify to me that the chosen are the ones who accepts and adheres to the calling of God.

That's why the Bible tells us in 2 Chronicles 7:14 that "If my people, who are called by my name, will humble themselves, pray, seek my face, and turn from their wicked ways, then will I hear from heaven and will forgive their sin and will heal their land." And what we must understand is that when we accept the purpose of God in our lives, there are certain things that come with the territory.

It amazes me how we tend to want to be chosen by God but shy away from what comes along with being chosen. That's why we can't take it personal when we start seeing our enemies for who they truly are, it comes with territory; we can't get discouraged when affliction knocks on our door; it just comes with the territory; we can't get frustrated when difficulties call our name, it just comes with the territory.

In 1 Peter chapter 4 verse 12 declares to us to think it not strange concerning the fiery trails which comes to try you, as if is some strange thing has happened to you. In other words, it's not by coincidence. And I've come to conclude that if God choose you to go through it, he has then anointed you to come out of it. That's why you can go through certain things that others can't and still come out winning, still come out with your right mind, still come out alive. Why? Simply because you've been chosen by God.

One thing I've come to realize that chosen people are peculiar people. A peculiar individual is referred to as someone who is strange, unusual, and abnormal. This further indicates to me that when God chose you, he has then anointed you to stand out.

The Bible tells us in 2 Corinthians chapter 6 verse 17 to come out from among them and be separated.

When you are chosen by God, you cannot expect for everybody to understand you, you can't expect everybody to accept you. Why? Simply because of who God has made you and the purpose he has placed inside of you. And if I can be honest with you, being chosen at times doesn't always feel good because we are humans, we all have a tendency to want to feel apart or feel accepted; and if we can be honest with ourselves, it doesn't always feel good being ostracized from society. It doesn't always feel good feeling misunderstood at times. It doesn't always feel good being judged and scrutinized. It doesn't always feel good felling alone and by yourself. But one thing I realized is that when God has detached you from the world's standards, it simply means he has a greater destiny designed for your life. And all I'm trying to tell somebody is that if God has called you out, that simply mean that He's calling you up.

If you've ever been on an airplane, the first thing they do is do a bag check because they realize that the higher you go, the less weight you can carry. I tell you that this is why God has separated you from certain people, places, and things simply because everybody can't go where you are going. You can't just go anywhere simply because of the great calling God has upon your life. The Bible tells us to lay aside every weight. Don't take it personally when God begins to isolate you from what once accepted you because I found out that separation is just an indication of elevation.

I've concluded that because God has chosen us, he's equipped us with everything that's needed to fulfill the task that he has set out for us to do. Everything that we need is already embedded on the inside of us, and because of this very notion, the enemy tends to play on the emotions of the people of God and tries to force us to believe what God has placed on the inside of us is insufficient, in which at times can cause feelings of inadequacies and uncertainties within ourselves.

This was the case with young Jeremiah. He felt because of his young age, he hadn't experienced enough for what God had called him to do, but God had reminded him that he chose him to be a prophet to the nations. Moses also fell victim to this very thing. The Bible tells us that because of his speech, he felt as though he wasn't capable of his assignment, but God had reminded him that he chose him to bring a nation out of captivity.

I've come to the conclusion that the only reason the devil fights who you are is simply because of WHO YOU ARE in which further proves that you pose as a threat to his kingdom. But I come to find out that every time the enemy tells us who and what were not, is an opportunity for God to prove him whose and what we are.

Let's stop underestimating what God has placed on the inside of us. The Bible tells us that we are made in the image of God; so therefore, if we are created in his image, part of him lives on the inside of us, and the word tells us that greater is he that is in me than is in the world. Therefore, since he lives on the inside of us, it further proves to the enemy and every last one of those against you that you are a force to be reckoned with.

And I come to encourage somebody when I tell you that if God is for you, who can be against you? His hand is in your life, that means you win!

CHAPTER 2
BROKEN BUT STILL VALUABLE

A woman in that town who lived a sinful life learned that Jesus was eating at the Pharisee's house, so she came there with an alabaster jar of perfume. As she stood behind him at his feet weeping, she began to wet his feet with her tears. Then she wiped them with her hair, kissed them and poured perfume on them. When the Pharisee who had invited him saw this, he said to himself, "If this man were a prophet, he would know who is touching him and what kind of woman she is—that she is a sinner."

—Luke 7:37–39

As individuals, we all have something that we deal with. I don't care how long you have been saved, I don't care how much you quote scripture, I don't care how many times you walk through those church doors, we all have something that we struggle with. And because of this, the enemy tends to use our issues and our proclivities as a way of trying to cause us to feel inadequate or unworthy of the calling of God on our lives. But I suggest to you that even with those issues, even with those struggles, God still has purpose on your life. I tell you that just because you have past, just because you have some hang-ups and some hookups, just because you have some struggles, does not make you any less valuable. What you're dealing with does not eliminate you from being used by God.

God still used Moses even though he had a speech impediment; he still used Thomas even though he knew he was a doubter; even though David was a murderer and an adulterer, after the fact, he still called him a man after his own heart. And this further lets me know that it does not matter what it is you may have done but what does matter is your ability to yield your will to God.

The enemy wants us to believe that because of our inadequacies, that our destiny is no longer valid. We then begin to identify ourselves with our issue. But I want to encourage you when I say that you are not your struggle! Your issue does not define your destiny.

God told Jeremiah that the thoughts he had toward the people of God are thoughts of good and not evil to give you and I an expected in. In other words, in spite of what I'm dealing with, in spite of what I may struggle with, God's desire for my life is to still bring me to a prosperous and successful finish. And I come to tell that your purpose is far greater than your struggle. Fact of the matter is, what's on the inside of you supersedes what you're dealing with!

God has placed something special within each and every one of us. I don't care whatever state you're in. There is still something significant within you that God has purposed for the advancement of the kingdom.

One of the enemy's main objectives is to blind us from the fact that God has a plane for our lives. You ever notice that every time you try to move forward toward God, there's always something trying to remind you of what you use to do and how you use to be or trying to give you reasons of why you're not qualified to be used by God? And to many times, do we allow the dealings of our past struggles or even in our current circumstances to hinder us from the purpose on our lives. But one thing I love about God is that he uses these things as a way of qualifying us to help somebody else. The Bible says that we overcome by the blood of the lamb and the word of our testimony. In other words, in order to bring somebody out of a situation, you have to be able to relate. I don't know about you, but I don't want anyone trying to talk to me if you never been through nothing. Don't try to talk to me because you don't know my struggle. How can you possible try to tell me how to come out and you never been in? But I need somebody to talk to me from a realistic point of view and tell me, "Yeah, I have been there," "Yeah, I have done that," and "Yup, I bought the T-shirt," and if God can do it for me, he can do the same for you!

As we enter the text, here it is now:

We see Jesus at the home of Simon the Pharisee, where he is eating and fellowshipping; and here enters a woman by the name of Mary. The Bible now speaks of three different Marys in particular. You have Mary the mother of

Jesus, you have Mary the sister of Martha, and then you have this particular Mary in whom this text is referring to.

Many theologians have identified this woman to be Mary Magdalene; however, the Bible does not give this woman any further identification other than the fact that she was a sinful woman. What we must understand is that although similar, this text is recounting a different situation.

This Mary wasn't like the rest of the Marys. She wasn't pure and holy like Mary, the mother of Jesus. She didn't sit at the feet of Jesus like Mary, the sister of Martha. On the contrary, this Mary had a past.

Many described her as a wicked woman. Some portrayed her to be harlot or a modern-day prostitute. But one thing I admire about this woman is that no matter what she had done and no matter who they said she was, even in the state that she was in, she somehow, someway found her way to Jesus. She knew she would be talked about. She knew she would be looked at crazy despite the opinions of others. She found her way to Jesus. This woman knew that whatever she needed wasn't in man, but it was in the presence of the Lord! And I don't care who you are and how long you have been saved, you can never come into the presence of God and leave the same way you came.

There's something about being in his presence. When I'm in his presence, I don't have to pretend I'm perfect. I don't have to pretend that I got it all together. When I'm in his presence, I can expose the real me. I don't have to put on facades, but he takes me with my struggles, he takes me with my issues, he takes me with my hang-ups, he takes me as I am, and he calls me his very own. Thank God for his presence!

As Mary comes to Jesus, she brings an alabaster box, and the Bible says it contained princely perfume. The people around Jesus began to feel some type of way. They couldn't understand how a woman of her caliber and of her essence could have the audacity and the unmitigated gall to come in the presence of Jesus. I can imagine the conversation went something like this. How dare she comes to Jesus knowing that she is a sinner and she got some problems? But isn't it funny that the main ones that claim to be so close to Jesus or the main ones that are keeping certain people away from Jesus?

In this case, the Pharisees were trying to find fault in Jesus, but then Jesus began to talk about the importance of forgiveness and compassion. These two things are the missing element in the Church. This is why, instead of people running to the church, they are running away from the church because of judgmental attitudes.

The first time we see somebody that doesn't look like the Church or act like the Church, instead of praying for them, the first thing we want to do is put them out of the church. Instead of praying for deliverance, we ostracize them! Can I tell you that the spirit of self-righteousness is killing the church, the perception of what true Christianity represents is killing the church?

For too long, society forced us to believe that Christianity is no more than coming to church and quoting scriptures and forgetting to teach us the value of true compassion. You may not look like everybody else, you may not talk like everybody else, you may not dress like every-one thinks you should dress, but there's still great value in you. Instead of the Pharisee seeing this woman's heart, they saw her issue instead of them seeing her soul. They saw her spirit instead of them seeing her needs. They focused on her faults. Through the adversity, she managed to get to Him. This woman desired forgiveness, but the Pharisees couldn't look past her issues.

Too many times, do we have to mention that people are coming to church, but we focus more on their prob-lems than their deliverance? We focus more on what they're wearing than their salvation?

And with the case of Mary, Still, Mary proceeded to Jesus. She came to him with this alabaster box full of per-fume. And if I could use my sanctified imagination, I can imagine that this box was closed so they couldn't necessar-ily see what was inside. But because it was a fragrance, it carried an odor. In other words, they couldn't see what was in it. They could only smell it.

And I come to tell somebody that people may not be able to see the value in you right now, but God said, "They are going to be able to sense it! You are going to walk in a room, and folks are going to know you carry that oil. You are going to places, and people are going to say stuff like, 'I don't know what it is, but there's just something about him.'"

I can't put my finger on it, but there's just something about her. And I come to tell somebody that you just need a diamond in the rough right now. People may not be able to see the significance in you right now, but after God takes you through the necessary process, the value God has placed in you is gone and shine greater than any setback, greater than any struggle, greater than any mistake, greater than any lie. Folks can tell. People think they know you, but they have no earthly idea. They haven't seen nothing yet!

Mary came to Jesus and then broke the alabaster box opened, and the Bible says she proceeded to wash Jesus's feet with her tears and then dried them with her hair, which is synonymous for worship and a sign of reverence.

In order to get what was inside the box, it had to be broken. In order for God to release the value within us, there has to be a breaking. Somebody's saying, "I don't understand what I'm going through. I don't get what's taking place in my life. I don't know why I'm struggling right now. I don't know why everything in my life is upside down. I don't know why my kids acting crazy."

God said, "I'm just breaking you to get the greatness out of you."

It is in the breaking that the anointing is released. It is in the breaking that God begins to prefects us. And I come to encourage somebody that your breaking is pushing you to your destiny. It may not feel good, it may not look good, but somebody's depending on what's inside of you. Your breaking is producing strength for somebody. It is releasing healing for somebody. It is releasing joy for somebody. Somebody needs what's on the inside of you.

What was so special about this encounter was the way Mary came to Jesus. She didn't come to him with hidden agendas or secret motives, but she came with a pure heart.

What we must understand is that, in order to have an encounter with God, there's away you have to come into his presence.

I've been found guilty of coming to church boggling down with the pressures of the world and not seeing the value of being in his courts. The Bible tells us to enter his courts with praise.

When I come into the presence of the Lord, I should have a premeditated praise. I should have a premeditated worship. We walk to the church as if it's an honor for us to be there. We come in as if God owe us something when, as the matter of fact, it's a privilege to be able to come into the house of the Lord!

Not only did Mary come into his presence with humility, but also she brought him something significant. Anytime we come into the house of God, we should come to him with a sacrifice. Whether it's of our time, talent, or treasure, whatever it is, when we come before God, there should be something valuable that we're offering up to our Lord and Savior!

Nowadays we take advantage of the presence of God. We treat Church like it's a chore and not understanding the true essence of being able to come before a faultless God! When I think about how God allows my imperfect self to come into his holy presence with my issues, with my struggles, with my proclivities, I dare not come into the house of God and act stick up. I dare not to come to his house and act like I got it all together. Every time I come through the door, my hands are lifted. Every time I come through the door, I'm going to give him every clap with my hands, every dance with my feet, every shout in my voice not because I'm so perfect but because I owe it to Him!

I would be remised if I didn't tell you that although God allows us to come to him in our broken state, it is not his will that we remain that way! The Bible says that whom the Son sets free is free indeed. It is not God's will that I remain bounded. It is not God's will that I remain in bondage. It is not God's will that I remain broken. God's desire for my life is for me to walk in total liberty! God is a God of restoration, and he desires to make us whole.

When I'm broken, I can only relate to your situation because I'm dealing with the same thing. But when I'm restored, that means I've been there, I've done that. And now I can not only relate but I can also tell you how to come out of it! The Bible says that many are the afflictions of the righteous, but God is able to deliver us from them all. I have to make up my mind that I want to be delivered. I have to be sick and tired of being sick and tired. I have to be tired of being bounded. I have to be tired of living in my mess, and when you're tired of something, you will do something about it!

I have come to the conclusion that the only reason we are not delivered because we don't want to be delivered. The Bible says that now unto him who is able to keep us from falling and present us faultless before God. I would hear the older saints saying, "He'll will keep you if you want to be kept!"

God loves us enough to where he'll take us as we are, but he loves us too much to leave us in the state that were in. But we have to want it for ourselves!

I want to encourage somebody when I tell you that God has purpose for each of our lives. I don't care what you've done, what mistakes you've made; you're still valuable to the kingdom. Too often we allow our issues to handicap us from our destiny. For too long, the enemy convinced us that because of our issues, we can't be used by God. But I come to set somebody free when I tell you that no matter what you deal with, God still has a calling on your life! The Bible says that we don't choose ourselves, but God chose us, which means in spite of me, he still chooses me! He knew I had problems when he chose me. He knew I had issues when he chose me. He knew I had some struggles when he chose me, still yet he chose me. The Bible tells us that there is no condemnation for those who are in Christ Jesus. It's time to step outside of guilt, shame, and brokenness and walk into your destiny!

CHAPTER 3
I'M NOT NORMAL, I'M ANOINTED

The Spirit of the Lord is upon me, because he has anointed me to proclaim good news to the poor, He has sent me to proclaim liberty to the captives and recovering of sight to the blind, to set at liberty those who are oppressed.

—Luke 4:18

I can recall a time when I first became a part of my church. One of the first sermons I heard preached from my pastor, he came from the topic, "I'm not normal, I'm anointed."

At the time I was a twenty-four-year-old young woman—who was shy, timid, and struggling to find who she was—when first coming to the ministry, I didn't have a true since of identity. I didn't quite know who I was or where I fit in. I just knew I wasn't like everybody else.

Everything about me was different. I didn't look like everybody else. I didn't talk like everybody else. My personality was different. My mannerisms weren't like everybody else. Even how I preserved things wasn't like everybody else;

and all these things, as a young adult, created insecurities and uncertainties within myself. I would often times try to blend in with the crowd because I didn't want my differences to be noticed. I would even go as far as asking God why couldn't I just be normal. But it was at the moment when I heard this particular word that God changed how I viewed myself and my purpose in God.

At that moment, I understood that God didn't need me to be like everybody else. He needed me to be a part for his glory. He didn't need me to sound like everybody else. He needed me to be the difference to those around me. He didn't need me to be normal but rather he needed me to be anointed.

When we look at the word *anointed*, it simply means "to be consecrated, set a part, or approved by God." And one thing I noticed in this particular text is that God doesn't just give us anointing is for vain purposes but rather for a particular work. The word tells us that God places his spirit on us and anoints us to proclaim his word, proclaim freedom to recover the sight of the blind and to set the captives free in which further indicates to me that wherever there is an anointing, there is also an assignment.

Can I help somebody when I tell you that God doesn't just anoint you to be idle but rather there is a work for you to do? And one thing I love about God is that he gives unconventional individuals, unconventional anointings to draw unconventional people. Can I help somebody when I tell you that there are certain people that are connected to you that only you have the ability to reach? There are certain places that only you have the ability to shift. That's why we can't afford to be the average day-to-day people, there has to be a difference because being normal won't release healing. Being normal won't bring deliverance. Being normal won't cause breakthrough. But the Bible declares that it is the anointing that destroys the yoke, and all I'm trying to tell somebody is that your anointing is necessary. You can't afford to be normal. You have to be anointed!

One thing I love about God is that he is not basing on his choice of anointing upon our perfection but rather he uses our hang-ups and our mess ups as a means of perfecting the anointing he has placed upon our lives.

Contrary to popular belief, you don't have to be perfect to be anointed. I'm talking to some people who have been through some stuff. I'm talking to some people who have made their share of mistakes. But despite all the hell you have been through, despite all the mistakes you may have made, despite all the things you may have lost—in spite of it all, you still got your anointing! And can I tell you that when God has anointed you, he then graces you to overcome certain things than the average person can't? Can I tell you why? It's because you're not normal, you are anointed. That's why after all you've been through, you still got your right mind, you still got your peace. It's because you have been anointed to survive.

The Bible says that in all these things, we are more than conquerors. Therefore, I'm convinced that if God has allowed you to go through it, he then has anointed you to come out of it, and when you come out, you're coming out with my hands up, you're coming out with more power, you're coming out with more grace because you've been anointed to go through it!

CHAPTER 4
IT'S NOT PERSONAL

Cry aloud, spare not, lift up your voice
like a trumpet and show my people their
transgression, and the house of Jacob their
sins.

—Isaiah 58:1

As a growing woman in God, I found that having people around you to hold you accountable and responsible is vital. Everyone needs that person or persons that can be honest with you. It was an author and fellow minister by the name of Norman Vincent Peale who wrote a book entitled *The Power of Positive Thinking*. And in this particular book, Minister Peale stated one of the truest and most relatable statements within our society to date. He simply stated that the problem with many of us is that we would rather be ruined by praise rather than saved by correction. I believe that this statement does not only bring truth to the world that we are living in, but it also brings clarity to a recurring issue that is affecting the body of Christ.

I have come to the conclusion that one of the biggest battles that we are facing within the church is notably against the spirit of offense. Many of us can attest the fact that we don't mind the admiration of the saints, we don't mind the pats on the back. We don't have a problem with being celebrated. We don't have a problem with being acknowledged. However, the issue comes about when what we think we know begins to be challenged.

Due to the advancement and modernization of our society, our generation has now gained a haughty and superior-type demeanor, and all of a sudden, nobody can't tell us nothing. We know it all, but can I help somebody when I tell you I don't care how modernized our world become? I don't care how many books you read. I don't care how many degrees you get. You still need somebody in your life that can correct you from time to time, somebody that won't sugarcoat nothing with you but that will tell you when you're off, somebody that will tell you when you are messed up. At the end of the day, you still need somebody in your life that can hold you accountable.

It amazes me how many of us will say that we want to be better and we want better but rather reject the correction that accesses us to better. Can I bless somebody when I tell you we can never go anywhere or achieve greater things in our lives until we learn how to stop taking correction so personal and learn how listen to somebody? It's not personal, it's purposeful!

Recently, my pastor began a series entitled, *Mastering Your Emotions*. Within this series, he began to talk about how at times we have the tendency of allowing our emotions to overtake us to the point that we react in our flesh instead of responding in the spirit. One thing our pastor mentioned to is that, although our emotions are necessary, they also must be appropriate correctly.

I have come to the conclusion that one of the main disadvantages of not properly defining and controlling our emotions is that we tend to take everything to heart. When ruled by our emotions, it hinders us from truly hearing the heart of something, and because of this, we now view everything from an egotistical standpoint and now every-thing is considered personal. The way someone looks at us is personal. The way someone speaks to us is personal. The way someone touches us is personal. We take correc-tion as personal. We take truth as personal. All the while, the intent may be innocent and a mean to benefit us, but because we're in our feelings, we take what was meaningless and innocent out of context and now the spirit of offence is birthed out all because we have not yet mastered nor taken control over our emotions. And now our biggest help becomes our biggest enemy.

When we look at this particular text, we see now the prophet Isaiah had been commissioned by God to go to the people of Zion to bring awareness of the hypocrisy of the people, particularly those who have been fasting and praying with impure motives. The people of Zion began to boast about their false since the fasting and praying but then began to blame God when they didn't see any man-ifestation in what they were doing. In other words, they wanted God's hand but not his heart because the hand is where the blessings flow, but when you have God's heart, it is when you take on the responsibility and obligation of a believer in the spirit of God.

I'sent that just like us church people. We want praise and recognition over what we are obligated to do by God. I don't understand. We want a pat on the back for tithing when you're supposed to tithe. We want a round of applause for coming to church when, in all actuality, it is our due diligence to God forsakes note to assemble. We want a standing ovation for praising God in tough times when, in reality, it is what we owe him to bless him at all times and to let his praises continue to be in our mouth. And can I tell you that this is why some of our blessings are being hindered? It's because our offerings to God are being done with ulterior motives. We're giving with motives. We're praying with motives. We're worshipping with motives, we're shouting with motives. But it was David who said, "God, create in me a clean heart and renew in me a right spirit."

Can I bless somebody when I tell you that if we're ever going to truly see the manifestations of God, we must first have a right spirit? Our hearts have to be pure, our spirits have to be pure, our reasonings have to be pure, and once our spirit is right we then won't have to coerce a blessing but rather blessing as the Bible says we will be added unto us. It's important that we check our spirit.

Here it is now in our featured verse:

God told Isaiah to go and warn the people of Zion of their ways. God told Isaiah that "Not only do I want you to go and tell them, but I need you to cry aloud and spare not." *Cry aloud* means "to be faithful, plain, and earnest in his approach," while *sparing not* which means "to not hold anything back."

Isaiah's assignment to the people of Zion was not to make friends. His purpose wasn't to be liked but rather his purpose was to say what thus said the Lord. God told Isaiah to raise his voice like a trumpet, which means with a loud voice, further indicates to me that he needed him to be aggressive in his approach.

And although I do believe God desires us to be wise and conscientious in our approach, I do not believe he called us to be passive. I believe that when God calls us, he calls us with a holy boldness, and what's taking place now in the body of Christ is that we have allowed personal feelings and relationships to cause us to lose our voice. We have become so concerned with our alliance to people that we are now forsaking truth, which is the word of God. We have now replaced truth with loyalty. We have replaced truth with being seeker-friendly, and now some of us have allowed that same loyalty to people to hinder our assignment with God. And can I tell you that this is why we have so many people dying and going to hell because we are forfeiting the truth?

We have too many people who are still bound because we are not telling them the truth. We have too many people that are locked up in their sins because we're not telling them the truth. The Bible says that it is the truth that shall set us free—not friendships, not relationships—but the truth. And you cannot tell me that you truly love somebody, and you want the best for them and you are not honest with them. And if you're anything like me, I don't believe you really love me if you're not real with me.

Every once in a while, I need somebody that will look past my feelings, look past my tears, pull me to the side, and tell me when I'm messing up. Tell me when I'm out of character. Tell me when I'm in my flesh because telling me the truth is the only thing that's going to make me better.

God now tells Isaiah to show the people their transgressions and their sins because it is in this revelation and in this truth that if received, will set them free. And one thing I've come to learn is that we have to stop taking truth so personal. The Bible says that "Open rebuke is better than secret love." And some of us have allowed correction to offend us to the point to where now it has stifled us in what God called us to do. We get rebuked and now we want to sing no more. We want to pray no more. We want to preach no more. You barely want to come to church, and some of us wonder why it seems as if there is no progression in our lives or it feels as if we're stuck in the same place year after year, time after time. Can I tell you why? It's because we have allowed offence to consume us to the point where now we're stuck living in the mundane.

But can I help somebody when I tell you that we will never become better, that we will never have better if we continue to stay paused in our offense? How oxymoronic of us to think that God will elevate us to another level. How can we expect God to prosper the works of our hands since we don't know how to properly take the correction? And all I'm trying to tell somebody is that once we get our hearts right, once we learn how to accept truth, and once we learn how to apply truth, there is no limit to what God will do. The Bible says that if we humble ourselves under the mighty hand of God, he then will exalt us in due season. And can I tell you that the same thing that we humble ourselves under, God will then cause us to prosper over?

Everything that is attached to you, God will then cause to be elevated—your money will be elevated, your business will be elevated, your family will be elevated all because you have come in alignment with the word of God!

CHAPTER 5
DON'T PANIC

Now a man named Lazarus was sick. He was from Bethany, the village of Mary and her sister Martha. [This Mary, whose brother Lazarus now lay sick, was the same one who poured perfume on the Lord and wiped his feet with her hair.] So the sisters sent word to Jesus, "Lord, the one you love is sick." When he heard this, Jesus said, "This sickness will not end in death. No, it is for God's glory so that God's Son may be glorified through it."

—John 11:1–4

Statistics have shown that 40 million of Americans which makes up about 18 percent of our population, mostly women, are being affected by anxiety. Anxiety is another form of fear or feelings of hopelessness, and if not dealt with properly, can cause depression, feelings of loneliness, and thoughts of suicide.

Another name for severe anxiety is what is known as panic attacks. Panic attacks are typically brought on due to extreme amounts of fear and worry. The Bible even goes as far as to quote the phrase "fear not" roughly 365 times. I personally don't believe that it's by coincidence that there is 365 days within a year.

One writer declared that God has given us a fear not for each day of the year. Although many of us understand that our trust should be rooted and grounded in God, many of us can testify that we have all one time or another, struggled in this area. I don't care how we are saved. There have been times where we have experienced feelings of concern—you worried about how that bill was going to get paid, you worried how you were going to make ends meet, you worried about that doctor's report. And despite how much faith we possess, there are times in this Christian walk with God where our faith will be tested.

Many times, our fear is brought due to our carnal mind trying to rationalize spiritual matters. The Bible even tells us that our ways are not his way and our thoughts are not his thoughts; and one thing I realized is that a lot of times, we can be so busy trying to understand God that we negate trusting God. Often times, especially as a believer, it is trying to use our carnal mind in an effort to rationalize the things we don't understand that can cause us to panic and move us outside of our faith and into desperation.

Many times, the enemy uses this as a source of fear when we can't seemingly justify what's taking place in our lives. It is in those moments when we don't know why we're in what we're in that at times cause distress. And if we all can be honest to ourselves, each of us has had a why moment with God.

You didn't understand the reason why you had to go through certain things. You didn't understand the reason why that particular thing had to happen to you of all people. After all, you, good people, you come to church, you try to live right, you pay your tithe, you really love God, and you just wanted to know why.

Anybody ever just wanted to know why because somehow if I knew the reason behind what I'm in, God would just somehow tell me the purpose behind what I'm in instead of just allowing me to go through it blind. Then maybe I could process it a little better. Yeah, I know in the end, it's going to benefit me. Yeah, I know in the end its going to work in my favor. Yeah, I know I'll understand it better by and by but right now. While I'm in it, I just want to know why!

It was once quoted by a well-known New York rabbi, Harold Samuel Kushner, who once stated that "Life is like a good book. The further you get into it, the more it begins to make sense." In other words, Rabbi Kushner believed that throughout the processes of life, the knowledge of what we experience in life will eventually be made clear. In other words, certain things are better understood with time. We get so bogged down in what we're in than we become motionless.

But can I help somebody when I tell you that if we are ever going to see the conclusion of our situation, we cannot afford to be stagnated in the process but rather we have to continually move while we're in it?

Here it is now, as we enter into the text, we see a familiar story.

We see two sisters, Mary and Martha, who resided in a small area called Bethany. This particular family had a fairly close relationship with Jesus until the point when he would come into the town and would reside with them. So it's quite obvious that when their brother Lazarus became sick, they would send word to Jesus. Seeing as they have a personal relationship with Jesus, after all, he's been to their home. He's eaten their food surely because of their relationship. It would seem that one word from them would send Jesus to their beckon call. This family was so close to Jesus to the point that the message that was sent to Jesus was even personalized when the messenger stated that the one in whom he loved was sick in which signified relationship.

All these further let me know that regardless to your relationship or status with God. There are some things he will still permit to take place in your life. Many of us can attest to the fact that, each of us could that there has been a period in each of our lives as believers where we have all been in situations that were contrary to our walk with God, although you're a tither and a seed sower, you've still found yourself having to struggle financially from time to time, although you come to church all the time, occasionally hell still hits your house.

Can I help somebody when I tell you that regardless of how saved you are, regardless of how many times you come to church, there are still some things in this walk with Christ that are inevitable! I hate to be the barrier of bad news, but your relationship with God does not make you the exception. Salvation does not make you exempt from trouble but rather it qualifies you. We all have to go through something.

Jesus now, who was leaving Jerusalem, gets the message from his dear friends concerning Lazarus. He heard it, sent message back that Lazarus would not die but that God would be glorified. Instead of Jesus immediately responding out of desperation of the needs of his friends, one would think after all, this is a matter of life and death, after all Jesus is now only two miles away in Jerusalem, after all it is his friend who is sick unto death. But the Bible says he was delayed for two more days.

And all these had brought me to the conclusion that our anxiousness or anxiety does not move God. Our tears and frustration do not move God but rather God moves according to his time. And many times, we, as believers, tend to take God's delay as his rejection. We become alarmed when we don't see a sudden move of God, but one thing I have come to learn is that God will sometimes delay us in order to reveal the true him because God does not operate in our time. What we deem as urgent, God has already fixed. But sometimes God allow you to feel the pressure of what you're in in order to reveal the true essence of who he is and to gain a greater appreciation of who he is!

Your delay may feel like denial, but it is really God's way of showing you a greater display of who he is. You've heard mama talking about him and you've heard daddy talking about him, but now through trials, now through experience, you now can personally say I now have experienced God and I have now experienced his power and now I know who he really is for myself.

After delaying for two days, Jesus is now ready to proceed to Mary and Martha. Seeing as just as few days prior, Jesus was being sought out to kill. His disciples were apprehensive of him returning to Bethany fearing that he would be exposed himself, as well as them. Yet Jesus felt it as necessary that it was time.

Thomas, unlike the other disciples, was willing to go wherever Jesus went even if it meant his life. Thomas declared that we may die with him.

And one thing I've learned is that sometimes God will put you in a rock and a hard place in order to test your alliance. He will allow things to happen just to test your loyalty. And I found out that if you really want to know the true nature of a person, just start going through with some stuff. You can always tell who's really with you when you start going through hard times.

When your money was good, they were with you. When your name was good, they were with you. But as soon as your money start acting funny, as soon as your name got dragged through the mud, all of a sudden, the ones you thought would be there, the ones you thought had your back, now you can't find them. I'sent that just like people?

How soon do we forget who was there when we needed them the most? How soon do we forget who was there to pray us through? How soon do we forget who helped pay our bills? How soon do we forget? Hardships test our alliance.

And one thing I've learned is that there are times when we are in a place of panic, we tend to search out other resources, other people, places, and things that are contrary to the will of God. What Thomas blessed him was that he was not concern about where he was leading to but his focus was who he was being led by.

Many times, panic or fear comes about when we take our focus off who's leading us. Isaiah tells us that God will keep us in perfect peace, whose mind is stayed on thee. A lot of times, we are so focused on the problem when God has already placed the solution in our face, but we can't see it because our focus is off to him.

Jesus now was headed to where Mary and Martha were. Lazarus had now been dead for about four days. It was accustomed within Jewish customs that the soul of the dead stayed near the grave for three days, and on that fourth day, there was no hope for resurrection. So Jesus knowing this waited until there was no life left in Lazarus. As a matter of fact, they had already buried Lazarus. So it would seem that it was the end.

Mary and Martha were now mourning the loss of their brother. They were being comforted by family and friends; and all of a sudden, Martha heard that Jesus was coming. And the Bible says that she slipped away from the crowd to meet him. This was a bit peculiar turn of events seeing as in a previous encounter, it was Martha who was concerned with keeping the house and it was Mary who was at the feet of Jesus, that it was Martha who was working and it was Mary who was worshipping; and now things had seemed to change.

Mary now was in the house while Martha was going to Jesus, and all of these had brought me to the conclusion that the enemy will use hardships as a way of changing our posture and position in God. We start worrying and we stop worshipping. We start panicking and we stop praising. The enemy's desire is to use these things as a way of drawing us away from God, whereas God's desire is to use it as a catalyst to draw us closer to him.

Martha saw Jesus, and she told him, "If you would have been here not if you would have come," which suggests that she desired his presence during the time of illness and not just after. My brother would still be alive.

Jesus then told her, "I am the resurrection."

Martha then called Mary to meet them. And she also told Jesus that if he was there, their brother would still be alive.

One thing I noticed is that they were so caught up in the presence of Jesus that they forgot about his ability. We, as believers, can become so consumed about when God will show up that we negate his capability and power. And can I tell you that it's not as important as to when he will show up, just as long as he shows up? Don't allow the current delay of your need to make you forget that he's still God. Even if he doesn't show up tomorrow, he's still able. If he doesn't show up next week, he's still able.

A song writer said, "He may not come when you want him, but he'll be there right on time because whenever he shows up, there shall be a performance!'

I'm convinced that he's an on-time God!

In the midst of this, they take Jesus to the grave that Lazarus is in. The Bible says Jesus began to groan, and at the other side of them was weeping. He wept in which it showed his compassion and sympathy for what has taken place. After all, this is his friend who's now dead.

Jesus was not only divine, but he was also human so quit naturally. He's grieving the loss of someone who was close to him. And one thing, I've come to learn that it is not just because God doesn't move on our accord doesn't mean he's not concerned. Just because he doesn't do what I want him to do when I want him to do it does not mean he doesn't care. Just because he permitted something to take place in my life doesn't mean he doesn't love me, but rather sometimes God loves me so much that he will allow certain things to happen so that I can know him and experience him in a greater way.

So Jesus now comes to the grave, and the Bible says he groaned the second time. This groaning was different from the first time.

The first groaning came from anger due to the lack of faith of those around him. This groaning however came from anguish.

Many theologians suggest that this groaning came as a result of Jesus seeing Lazarus in the grave as a type and shadow of his fate that was to shortly follow. Jesus then told them to take away the stone. They told him that since he's been dead for a while, there was a stench, and his body was badly decomposed. In other words, they are telling Jesus that there's nothing else that can be done; it's over.

And one thing I love about this is that while they were declaring it to be over, Jesus was preparing new life. What looked like death to them was actually a new beginning.

Jesus now told them that if they would only believe, they would see the glory of God. The word *believe* is heavily emphasized within this text due to the fact that before God can do anything in our lives, we must first believe in his power.

God's glory is contingent upon us believing. The Bible even tells us that all things are possible for those who believe. It is because we believe that miracles, signs, and wonders follow. It is because we believe that we are saved. It is because we believe that we are healed, delivered, and set free. There can be no possible manifestation without belief, and the enemy uses anxiety and panic as a way of stiffening our belief in God's ability.

When we can't fully process or understand what God is doing in our lives, we start taking matters into our own hands and relying upon our own ability and not God's. That's why I'm convinced that sometimes God has allowed us to go through some situations and things as an effort to strengthen our belief in him. Some of us wouldn't believe how we believe today if we never experienced some type of trouble. But because I know him, I believe in him.

The Bible says that after he told them to remove the stone, he began to pray. And in the midst of praying, he told God, "I know you hear me, but because of the people around me, I say these things so they may believe."

They now removed the stone, and Jesus told Lazarus to come forth. He got up from the grave at the command of Jesus, but he was bonded by the clothes he was buried in. Then Jesus told his grave clothes to loosen them.

The Bible says that "Many believed because they saw this happen."

I found the saying true that what we go through is not about us but for somebody else. Sometimes God has allowed us to go through some situations and things as a catalyst for somebody else's belief.

I was reading a book entitled *Instinct: The Power to Unleash Your Inborn Drive* by Bishop T. D. Jakes; and in the book, he talks about a time when he got laid off his job. He says he couldn't afford to panic because he had a family that was depending on him. So instead of being afraid, he became resourceful. He started a lawn care company, and through this, he was not only able to provide for his family, but he was able to show his children that you can overcome any situation.

I want to encourage somebody when I tell you that some people only believe because they've seen you overcome. Some people only believe because they've seen you go through and come out better. You are the evidence to somebody of what God can do, and they know if God did it for you, he can do it for them.

You are the proof of what the Lord can do. They're looking at a miracle and don't even know it. They're looking at a survivor and don't even know it. They're looking at an overcomer and don't even know it. If they want to know if God can provide, they can just look at you. If they want to know if God can heal, they can just look at you. If they want to know if God can make a way, they can just look at you! You are the proof of what God can do!

CHAPTER 6
BY ANY MEANS NECESSARY

And a woman was there who had been
subject to bleeding for twelve years, but no
one could heal her. She came up behind
him and touched the edge of his cloak,
and immediately her bleeding stopped.

—Luke 8:43–44

When I was younger, I was heavily infatuated with the
African American culture and several different political
activists, such as Martin Luther King, Rosa Parks, Maya
Angelou, but one of my favorites just so happened to be
Mr. Malcom X.

During a time when our country was in racial disarray
as it is now during a 1968 founding rally, Mr. X quoted the
famous phrase that would be heard all over the world and
would later be detailed in his signature biography trans-
lated as "by any means necessary."

He stated this as a way of getting people to understand
that in order to see change, we cannot wait upon pleasant
conditions but rather action must be forced.

When we look at this text, Jesus had just healed the man with several demons. He was now crossing over to the other side of the lake, and as he got to the other side, he ran into a man by the name of Jairus. Jairus was now one of the leaders in the synagogue, and as he saw Jesus, the Bible says that he fell to his knees and told Jesus that his daughter was dying and needed him to come lay hands on her so that she may live.

As Jesus was proceeding with Jairus, the Bible says that a large crowd followed and pressed around him. Among this crowd, laid a woman who had been dealing with an issue of blood for twelve long years. This woman now was considered unclean, and as a result of her condition, she was automatically separated from society. The Bible says that she heard that Jesus was coming and she desired to be free from this affliction so she ended up going to where he was.

And one thing I can admire about this woman is that she was so desperate to be healed that she didn't wait on Jesus to come to her but rather she got up on her own accord and went to him. And too many times we miss out on our change or deliverance because we are too busy waiting on it to be initiated, we're too busy waiting on a word, we're waiting on somebody to call our name when the word is.

Faith without work is dead. We have to stop waiting on a change and start causing a change. We cannot expect our situation to progress while sitting idle. And the problem that we're facing in the church today is that we have too many lazy saints. It amazes me that we say we want things to be better; we want God to bless us indeed. God change this and change that but have a problem with meeting the requirements for change.

I told you that change can only take place when you first decide to change something.

So here it is now.

As this woman is among the crowd, one thing I can admire about her is that even though she was shunned from society due to what she was dealing with. This woman risked humiliation. She risked being exposed by still choosing to seek Jesus in a public place. And the reason is that some of us are still bound in what were in. It is because we are too ashamed about what we're dealing with.

A lot of times, we have a tendency of allowing the opinions of people, and our own selfish pride hinders what God is trying to change. And truth be told, a lot of us are not experiencing change nor ever will experience change until we learn how to get over people. We're too worried about what someone has to say. We are too concerned about what people think, and I can tell you that this is the reason so many people, especially our millennials, are now turning away from the church all because there's becoming a problem with transparency.

Nobody wants to be real about what they've been through. People are tired of hearing church rhetoric. People are tired of hearing a bunch of church clichés when some of them are struggling to survive. They need to hear something real.

Nowadays we are too busy waiting on somebody's approval that we end up missing out on what God is trying to do in our own lives. The Bible says that we overcome by the blood of the lamb and the word of our testimony. And I can tell you that the main reason why the enemy wants us to feel ashamed about what we're dealing with is because he understands the significance of your testimony. He understands that what God is doing for you is not just going to change your life but also change the life of somebody that is connected to you.

But we are too afraid of being transparent. We act as if we have it all together because we don't want nobody to know that although we are singing and shouting, we got issues too. Although we're smiling, we are still struggling. And one thing I've found out is that God sometimes deliver us openly, in order to heal somebody privately. Somebody needs to see a public display of what God can do!

As this woman had blended in with crowd, the Bible goes on to say that prior to this encounter, she spent everything she had on many physicians, but instead of getting better, she only got worse. And because she ran out of options and ran out of money, she then afterward decided to seek Jesus. And all these had helped me realize that the reason that some of us are stuck in the place we are in is because we have preferred our own way of doing things and our personal convenience and have consequently made God our last result.

The Bible says to "Seek ye first the kingdom of heaven, and all these things shall be added unto you." But we have it backward. If our way don't work out, then we seek God. If our relationship don't work out, then we seek God. If our jobs don't work out, then we seek God.

Although Jesus was not this woman's first choice, she believed that there was still hope for her situation, which was evident by her continuous pursuit for twelve years for her healing which caused her to seek the help of other physicians to cure her ailment.

After many failed attempts, she heard about Jesus and made up her mind that if she could just touch the hem of his garment, she would be made whole, which suggests to me that her faith wasn't the problem but it was who she put her faith into. Too often do we waste the time and energy looking to people and things to be our saving grace, and we end up missing out on the power of God.

I don't believe that it's by coincidence that although there were people closer to Jesus than this woman was, she happened to be the only one healed while others were concerned with the personality of Jesus; she just wanted to experience his power. This woman didn't care about how close she was to Jesus; she just wanted contact.

Can I help somebody when I tell you that a personality can't heal you? A personality can't deliver you, but it's only by the power of God. And when you are in a position where you really need God to change some stuff, you don't care about what somebody got to say. You don't care what you got to do. You don't care where you got to go. But all you know is that if I can, just get to God! You can say whatever you want about me but just let me get to God. Classify me as whatever you want but just let me get to God because everything I need is in the presence of the Lord. Just let me get to him!

This woman now—not only heard about Jesus, but in order to touch him—had too positioned herself among the crowd going in the direction in which he was going. In order for her to be healed, she couldn't be around with those who were in the same condition as her. In other words, she knew she couldn't be healed staying where she was. She knew she had to go where it wasn't normal for people such as herself to go. And when this woman decided to change her position, she was then able to get to where Jesus was.

And the Bible says that when she touched the hem of his garment, she was instantly made whole. The word *instantly* or *immediately* is the most frequently used word in the book of Mark, which means that at once she was healed.

This suggests to me that her healing wasn't just about her faith but also about her being at the right place at the right time. And a lot of us are not experiencing change because some of us are out of position. We want God to turn our situation around, but we're not willing to sacrifice some stuff. It amazes me that we want God to change the state that were in while we are yet living outside his will. We want God to bless what he didn't ordain. God blesses my relationship when he didn't put it together. God blesses my career when he didn't call you to that field.

But I can help somebody when I tell you that before God changes anything, there are some people, places, and things we must first rid ourselves of. This is why God has to separate you from certain people, places, and things simply because everybody is sent a part of your assignment.

The Bible tells us to lay aside every weight. Don't take it personal when God begins to isolate you from what once accepted you because I found out that separation is just an indication of elevation. That's why you are feeling alone right now. That's why you are feeling by yourself right now because before God can change you, he has to first change your atmosphere.

I don't believe that it was by coincidence that this particular woman had been suffering with this condition for twelve years, and that Jairus's daughter was also twelve. The number twelve is simply significant because it represents God's power and authority.

Our pastor preached a few Sundays ago that God was bringing us to our conjunction in which is a place where our purpose and our condition will amend, which we will have the ability to give our condition direction. And I realized that many of us will remain in our situation until we learn how to utilize the power that is within us to shift us.

The Bible tells us that God has given us power and dominion. In which further lets me know that we don't have to stay in the situation that we're in but rather God has given us the power to change our conditions. But because many of us have become comfortable in our situation, we have now become stagnant, and I can tell you that anything that is stagnant for too long will eventually die.

One thing that bothers me the most is that God has given us power, but we let it lie dormant. We have become too mundane to our situation to the point that we allow the power that God has given to us, as believers, to lie in waste.

There are too many believers that are dying sick, too many believers dying broke, too many believers dying struggling when we have the power to change our situation. God has given us power. It's up to us to use it!

I admire this woman because not only did she position herself to be healed, but she also didn't allow her condition to determine her result.

A lot of us have been guilty of allowing our situation or our issue to tell us what we can have and who we can be, and we end up missing out on the things of God! But I come to encourage somebody when I tell you that although you may be in a situation, that situation is not you. Your condition may be on you, but it's not in you!

There was a documentary on TV by a famous producer and actor Tyler Perry.

In the interview, Mr. Perry spoke about his childhood of growing up in a poor household in New Orleans. He went on to talk about many series of events within his childhood and some of the abuses he was subjected to, but one thing that stuck out to me within the interview was when he said that even as a kid, he knew where he was seasonal. Although he was poor, he knew it wouldn't last always. Even though he was being abused, he knew it wouldn't last always.

Can I help somebody when I tell you that you are not what you're going through, you're just going through a season? You are not broke, you're just going through a season? You are not alone, you're just going through a season? You are not broken, you're just going through a season?

The Bible tells us that "Weeping may endure for a night, but joy cometh in the morning." Get ready for your morning!

CHAPTER 7
DO SOMETHING DIFFERENT

Immediately he made the disciples get into the boat and go before him to the other side, while he dismissed the crowds. And after he had dismissed the crowds, he went up on the mountain by himself to pray. When evening came, he was there alone, but the boat by this time was a long way from the land, beaten by the waves, for the wind was against them. And in the fourth watch of the night he came to them, walking on the sea. But when the disciples saw him walking on the sea, they were terrified, and said, "It is a ghost!" and they cried out in fear. But immediately Jesus spoke to them, saying, take heart; it is I. Do not be afraid." And Peter answered him, "Lord, if it is you, command me to come to you on the water." He said, "Come." So Peter got out of the boat and walked on the water and came to Jesus.

—Matthew 14:22–29

In the book entitled *Successful Women Think Differently: 9 Habits to Make You Happier, Healthier, and More Resilient*, by an author and life coach, Valorie Burton explains that there are two different types of mind-sets we all operate in: the first one is what physiologist calls a "fixed mind-set," and the other is what is known as a "growth mind-set."

She goes on to explain that a person who is operating in a fixed mind-set believes that change is not inevitable. In other words, a person with a fixed mind-set believes that things are destined to be the way they are. On the contrary, she describes a person who is operating in a growth mind-set as someone who understands that in order for them to grow in one's life, change has to take place.

And one thing I have come to realize is that one of the biggest issues that we deal with in the church and the killing of the body of Christ is the spirit of complacency.

Complacency is another form of stagnation. It is when you are satisfied or contented living in a mediocre condition.

Can I help somebody when I tell you that although God does desire for us to be contented in what he allows us to go through, it is not his will for us to get comfortable because where we are, where God has positioned you at this present time is merely temporary? And the problem with some of us is we have turned what was supposed to be seasonal into our permanent position. And once we get comfortable in a situation, what happens now is we start doing things out of habit and not of expectation! We start giving out of habit. We start praising God out of habit. We start praying out of habit, and we lose our sense of expectation for greater.

Nowadays we are living in a society that has become comfortable living in the status quo. We don't want to rock the boat so we rather live comfortable lives rather than challenging our surroundings. We have become comfortable with being sick. We have gotten comfortable with being broke. We have gotten comfortable working nine to five, and we began to settle for the way things are and not by what the word has declares it can be.

Because we have gotten so lackadaisical, God will sometimes cause things to happen in our lives to make us so uncomfortable to the point where it will force us to change what's around us. For most of us, comfort signifies security, and it gives us a false since of control. But it was Albert Einstein who famously quoted the phrase: "A ship is always safe on shore, but that is not what it was built for."

Can I help somebody when I tell you that God's purpose for our lives exceeds where we are and in order for us to experience the fullness of God, it's going to require us stepping out from what is safe and going into unfamiliar territory?

In this season, God is calling us to unusual places, and I believe that if God is calling us to uncommon places, it means he has orchestrated an uncommon blessing.

Lately, some of you have found that God is challenging you more than the average. He is challenging you more in you who are giving than the normal. He is challenging you more in your prayer time than the normal. Can I tell you why? He challenge you more than the usual simply because what he has prepared for you is not for the average. And can I prophesy that about three people would tell you that this next move of God won't be normal? What God is about to do for the body of Christ, we won't be able to explain it.

Here now: Jesus had just finished teaching and feeding the multitude of five thousand. The people had never experienced someone like Jesus or his miraculous power before, so naturally, there is now an even greater demand for Jesus. I can imagine the crowd getting aggressive to the point now Jesus had to separate himself from his disciples in an effort to steal away from the crowd.

He then told his disciples to get on the boat and meet him on the other side. As they were on their way to meet Jesus, they encountered some turbulent winds. The Bible says that the winds were contrary which meant it was conflicting with their destination to get to Jesus.

And can I tell you that every time God challenges us to change the status quo of a thing, there will always be an opposing force that comes to hinder the progress of your assignment?

The Bible talks about the story of Nehemiah and how he built the wall in Jerusalem, and here came two men by the name of Sanballat I and Tobiah who sent to hinder the work of the Lord.

Can I tell you that the enemy's whole agenda is to obstruct you from your assignment because your assignment is a caution to his defeat so he would send counterattacks such as doubt. He sent attacks such as fear. He sent attacks such as discouragement as an effort to deter you from your God-given assignment.

But one of the things I realized is that it is not the beginning of a thing the enemy fights most because notice in the beginning of your assignment that you have a lot of zeal. You have a lot of tenacity. You are optimistic, but it is when you are the closest to your destination when the enemy begins to fight your endurance the most.

Many of us can testify that when God first called us to our divine place with him, there was a certain excitement we had. You were excited about prayer. You were excited about serving. You were excited about singing. You were enthusiastic about your business, but somewhere in the middle of life's adversities and disappointments, we could somehow lose that same vitality that we've once had.

Bishop T. D. Jakes once stated that the toughest times in life are not in the beginning of the struggle, but it is when you're the closest to the shore when you're more vulnerable to collapsing.

Can I help somebody when I tell you that the enemy doesn't want your beginning but rather he wants your ending? It wasn't until the disciples got close to their destination that the storm begins to oppose them the most, and all I'm trying to tell somebody is that whenever there is a greater level of intensity in what you're enduring, can I prophesy and tell you that the end of your struggle must not be too far off? That's why you've been fighting like you're fighting. That's why some of us have been struggling on a greater level lately. But I want to encourage you when I tell you that it's almost over!

As we venture back to the story, what we must notice is that this was not the disciple's first time experiencing such an encounter like this before.

In this same book of Matthew chapter 8 verse 23, it talks about how these same disciples experienced another storm. While this is taking place, Jesus was now at the bottom of the ship sleeping. They woke him up, told him about what's going on, and he came to the top of the ship and spoke peace to the winds and to the storm. And the Bible says that the storm began to calm.

I began to ask God, "Why did you put them in two different storms almost simultaneously? Has anybody ever felt like you are constantly going through something? Like Job, you can't seem to catch your breath. You come out of one thing, and it seems like something else happens, and you are trying to figure out what's going on."

But can I tell you that each encounter, God allows us to go through different purpose? God begins to show me that although these two encounters were similar, the circumstances were different. Understand that in this particular situation, they didn't have the comfort of having Jesus physically on the boat with them. Not only Jesus was not physically with them, but in the previous storm, they also had the comfort of having daylight, but this time, it was now completely dark, in which caused the disciples to fear even more. Due to their previous encounter by now, the disciples had become familiar with storms.

And one thing I've found out is that any time, God is trying to get you to somewhere greater. One thing, he begins to do is to challenge what has become familiar, and any time God begins to challenge your familiarity. It typically signifies that you have outgrown where you are. I have noticed within the Church is that a lot of us would rather remain in a place we have outgrown and unproductive then to be stretched beyond our comfort zone. Can I tell you why? Because when God begins to stretch you. It also requires another level of responsibility. It requires another level of accountability.

God begins to require more of your time. He requires more of your talents. He requires more of your treasure. And I've found out that the saying is true that if you want something you never had, you have to eventually do something you've never done. Can I prophesy to those individuals who God is challenging in this season when I tell you that any time God is requiring more of you, it's because he's trying to get more to you? He's trying to get something out of you to get something to you!

As the story goes on, the disciples were now enduring these turbulent winds. They were now about 670 feet away from shore. And the Bible says that it is now the fourth watch of the night, which gives the time to be about 3:00 a.m. It is now completely dark. And the Bible says they saw a presence walking on water and assumed that it was a ghost; they began to fear.

This signifies to me that what caused them to fear was not necessarily the storm in itself but fear arose in their inability to see while in the storm. Many of us can testify that it's one thing challenged by God when you can seemingly see the outcome of the situation. But what do you do when God begins to challenge you to do something unfamiliar and you can't see your way out of it?

There's a backup plan. There's no plan B.

What do you do when God challenges you, and it doesn't make sense?

God tells you to sow, and you get this cut-off notice. (It just doesn't make sense.) God says you're healed, but you're still feeling symptoms. (It just doesn't make sense.) God tells you to love your enemy, but they constantly are running your name through the mud. (It just doesn't make sense.)

Because it was dark, it did not only hinder the disciples' sight, but it also hindered them from recognizing Jesus. They couldn't recognize the presence of Jesus; they could only hear his voice.

Jesus told them to fear not for it was while the other disciples sat afraid; it was Peter who began to petition Jesus asking to bid him to come on the water. Jesus then said one word, in which was "come."

The word *come* is significant because it was Jesus giving Peter an access or approval to walk on what was trying to overtake them, and God told me to tell somebody that in this season, he's giving you access to whatever have tried to hinder your assignment. He's giving you an access with banks. He's giving you an access with investors. He's giving you an access to new doors. God said access granted because they couldn't recognize Jesus! They had to now depend on their hearing.

The book of John tells us in the tenth chapter that my sheep hear my voice, and I know them, and they follow me. And when God had made you a game changer. You are not moved by what you see, but rather you are empowered by what you hear.

The Bible tells us that faith is the substance of things you hoped for and evidence of things not to be seen. Because in all actuality, if we operate based on what we saw at times, some of us wouldn't even be here right now.

I do believe that we can all testify that at times, our reality has a way of overshadowing our faith because, at times, what we see can contradict on what we hear.

But one thing I've come to learn is that although my reality doesn't always align with what I hear, it is my obedience that predicates my manifestation. And all I'm trying to tell somebody is that if you obey what you hear, you will soon see what he said. The Bible says that if we are willing and obedient, we shall eat the good of the land. We just have to do what he said!

Jesus now told Peter to come, and he was now walking on the water and noticed that while Peter was walking on the water, not once did Jesus rebuke the storm as he did in the chapter 8. He didn't divide the water as what he did with Moses, but rather he gave Peter the power and authority to walk on it. The Bible says that Jesus told the disciples to meet him on the other side, which suggests to me that Jesus, being an all-knowing God, knew that the storm they were about to experience still purposely sent the disciples to Capernaum without him. This suggests to me that there are some things God has allowed us to go through, allowed us to experience to show us our true ability.

And one thing about God is that he won't always take you over it, but he will give you the power to go through it. He won't always stop it, but he will empower you to endure it. Can I help somebody when I tell you that whenever God is birthing out something different in you, you will experience your share of adversity? You will experience your share of criticism. You will experience your share of doubters. You will experience your share of struggle. And the problem that we face today is that we are too busy looking for confirmation from people to fulfill the assignment God called us to do.

And can I help somebody when I tell you that you don't need validation from people when you have word from the Lord? Stop waiting on people to approve your business. Stop waiting on people to approve your ministry. Stop waiting on people to approve your ideas. Stop waiting on people to approve your ambitions because some people will forever be satisfied with you being stuck on the boat afraid with them.

That's why you can't expect everybody to support you. Stop expecting everybody to back your vision because, truth be told, everybody won't understand your assignment, and we have to stop getting so easily offended when we don't get the response or support we desire because at the end of the day, it is the call that God has given to you to fulfill and not them.

Pastor preached a sermon not too long ago about, "It's my assignment and not yours." So even if they don't support, you still have an obligation. Even if they don't come, you still have an obligation. Even if you have to accomplish it by yourself, you still have an obligation! Wipe your eyes, square your shoulders, and get the job done.

As Peter was walking on the water, he was getting closer to Jesus. And as he was getting closer, the Bible says that he began to notice the storm. And as he focused on the storm, he began to sink. As he was sinking, he told Jesus, "Save me." The Bible says instantly, "Jesus reaches out his hand and caught him and while the other disciples are watching on while Peter is sinking."

I can imagine that some of them questioned Peter's actions. But one thing I love about it is that not only did they have to watch him sink, but they also had to watch him stand.

Can I tell you that some people are watching you from a distance trying to see if you are gone failing, trying to see if that idea worked out, trying to see if that business is still running? But I got good news: the Bible says that "Whosoever believeth on him shall not be ashamed."

I want to prophesy to everyone who is reading this that I tell you that they may see you stumble, but God said they want see you fall.

CHAPTER 8
IT'S YOUR TIME!

Jesse had seven of his sons pass before Samuel, but Samuel said to him, "The Lord has not chosen these. So he asked Jesse, "Are these all the sons you have?" "There is still the youngest," Jesse answered. "He is tending the sheep." Samuel said, "Send for him; we will not sit down until he arrives." So he sent for him and had him brought in. He was glowing with health and had a fine appearance and handsome features. Then the Lord said, "Rise and anoint him; this is the one.
—1 Samuel 16:10–12

When we look at the word *time* as mentioned in the Webster's dictionary, it is described as "an indefinite continued progress of existence and events in the past, present, and future." It is also described as "the measured period during which an action, process, or condition exists or continues." It was quoted by a famous playwright, Tennessee

Williams that "Time is the longest distance between two places."

Time is the one thing here on earth that is not controllable and that cannot be altered. One thing about time is that it moves on its own accord. It is not accelerated due to anxiousness or anxiety but rather progresses in its proper element. The same can be said for time in the spiritual aspect because the Bible even declares that there is a season for everything.

And one thing that I realized is that so many times do we seek or desire things that contradicts the season or the time that were in. In other words, we are seeking things but don't possess the necessary tools or have the necessary things in place to maintain what we're seeking. We want prosperity but don't even have a bank account. We want CEO titles and positions but don't even want to further educate ourselves. And the problem that we are facing in the church is that instead of allowing time to take its natural course, we begin to go against our designed season. We have gotten so enthralled with our own personal desires that we negate the responsibility that's connected to what we're asking God for.

The Bible says that to whom much is given much is required. And can I bless somebody when I tell you that elevation comes when you are shown diligently over what you have been given charge over? The Bible says that if we are faithful over the few things, God will then make us ruler over many. We're asking God for many when we can't even produce with the few. We're asking God for increase, but we can't even grow with what we have. We're asking for enlarged territories when we can't even make an impact where we are! We have to work what we got!

One thing I love about time is that it is as mentioned earlier a continuous process. And quite often, when we think of time, we are thinking of it in a carnal aspect, which is referred to as *chronos*—the measurement of time by minutes and seconds. However, God measures time by *kairos*, which is an appointed time or an opportune moment. And can I help somebody when I tell you that there will come a point in your life when God will allow your *chronos* to meet your *kairos* in which the current place that you are in now will eventually collide with the promises of God on your life and will then shift you into your divine season? And what I love about God's designed season for our lives is that it cannot be compromised by the things of this world.

Our season is not moved or challenged by circumstances or by individuals, but when it's your time, what God has for you is inevitable! In other words, your situation can't stop it. Your haters can't hinder it. Bills cannot deter it. When it's my time and season, no devil in hell can stop what God is doing in your life. Somebody shouts glory!

Although it cannot be stopped, I would be remised it. I didn't tell you that it can be stagnated by lack of preparation. Too many times have we delayed our own season because we don't prepare for what we're seeking! And I realized that a lot of times, we're waiting on manifestation when, all the while, manifestation is waiting on us. But can I prophesy to somebody when I tell you that now is not the time to get lackadaisical? Now is not the time to lose your zeal? Because in this season that we are in, God is now releasing opportunities and moments greater than you and I have ever experienced but can be forfeited by not being ready! You can't afford to miss your moment!

Here it is now.

We saw a man by the name of Samuel. Samuel, who was introduced to us at the beginning of the text as the miracle son of a barren woman by the name of Hannah, has now been chosen by God to anoint Saul as king of Israel. After Samuel anoints Saul, time went on, Saul was now reigning as king; and so what happened now was God had a conversation with Saul and instructed Saul to go into battle with the wicked Amalekites. He then told Saul, "Not only do I want you to go into battle, but I want you to kill everything—kill the men, kill the women, kill the children, and even kill the animals. As a matter of fact, Saul, don't leave anything alive."

Saul now ended up going to war. But instead of adhering to God's instructions, he ended up preserving what he desired over what God initiated him to kill.

And can I tell you that God's timing is predicated upon us killing some stuff? And some of us wonder why we're still in the same place, why there seems to be no progression in our lives. Can I tell you why? It's because there are some things that are attached to us that requires death!

But the problem that we face today is that we try to resuscitate what's already been put in the ground. Before God can take us higher, there are some things that we must first release. Some of us are being delayed by relationships that need to be released. We are being hindered by some habits that need to be released. There are some connections that we need to release before a shift can take place. It is a dangerous thing to hold on to what God has taken his hands off!

God now told Samuel to go to Bethlehem and to anoint one of Jessie's sons as king of Israel, and he would know God's chosen by the tilting of the oil.

As Samuel entered into the city, he saw Jessie and invited him and his sons to the special sacrifice. As they began to partake in the festivities, Samuel was now noticing the sons of Jessie. The first son he took notice of was Eliab. Eliab had a structure like a king, and because he looked the part, Samuel was sure he was God's chosen, but looks can be deceiving. Samuel was too busy judging his characteristics but not discerning with his character; and a lot of times, if he walks, talks, or looks like God, we automatically think he's God chosen. But just because they know scripture doesn't mean it's God. Just because they know how to speak in tongues doesn't mean it's God. Just because they're wearing a suit and tie doesn't mean it's God, and the problem with the church is that we have allowed charisma to overshadow character, we have allowed gifts to take precedence over the anointing. And now God said, "It's time for the church to get back to discerning!"

God had reminded Samuel that the difference between him and a man is that he didn't choose someone based on appearance but rather by the countenance of their heart. And what the enemy does is he will try and give us preconceived notions of what our time and season are subjected to base on someone else's experience.

Samuel had a predetermined perception of what a king was based on his experience with Saul, but what we must remember is that the people chose Saul and not God. And a lot of us are judging our moment or season through situations that are man-made and not God ordained.

All I'm trying to tell somebody is that this next move of God won't make since to the carnal mind, but it will produce a miracle for the spirit. What God is about to do for the church won't be able to explain it. The way God is about to bless you just won't make sense.

God now had just told Samuel that he had rejected Eliab. Jessie continued to bring forth each one of his sons, yet each of them where rejected!

Samuel now asked Jessie if there were any other sons. Jessie made mention that he had one more son by the name of David, but he was in the field tending to the sheep.

David entered the room, and what I found to be interesting is that, in the beginning of the text, Samuel told Jessie and his sons to consecrate themselves before the sacrifice. But here was David who had just come in from the field. His father told Samuel that he was a bit ruddy but not once was David asked to go through the same consecration as his brothers, but rather as soon as he entered the room, the Bible says that oil instantly began to till.

And what I love about God is that, when it's your time and season—instead of you having to go through the normal formalities than others may had endured—he will do is give you a quantum leap, which means God will give you divine advancement!

And God told me to tell somebody not to get used to where you are now because he's about to accelerate every area of your life. What took some people years to accomplish is what only takes you a matter of months. God said to my people that he's about to take you to heights where eyes have not seen nor ears have heard nor have it entered into the hearts of man! Why don't you touch about three people and tell them neighbor God is about to speed up the process?

One thing I realized is that although David's anointment may have seemed to be accelerated, no one recognized his time serving! David had to wait approximately fifteen years from the time he was first anointed by Samuel to the time he became king of Judah. It was another seven years before David was anointed as king all over the Israel.

This means that David waited over twenty years of his life to be a king. I'm talking to people where individuals see you, and they think you got to where you are overnight. They think your success was handed to you on a silver platter, but if they only knew the work you put in, if they only knew the tears you shed, if they only knew the times you were looked over, if they only knew the process you had to endure, they see your glory but can't even fathom your story. If they only knew, it came with a price!

What I love about the story is that although David didn't look like a king, he didn't talk like a king nor did act like a king, but God still chose him as a king. Although David's brothers had the experience and stature of a king, David had God's heart.

And I come to the realization that a lot of us are missing the time and season God has for our lives simply because we have ulterior motives. We have our own agendas and not God's. Some of us desire new levels for vain causes and reasons and not for the uplifting of the kingdom.

Can I bless somebody when I tell you that the reason God calls us into greater times and seasons in our lives is not for our own sake but because there is an assignment that's connected to where he's calling us to? And a lot of times, we can get so focused on the applause of the people that we miss the purpose of the assignment. But if we can ever stop making our assignment about us, your assignment is not about having the biggest platform, it's not about how many people you can make buck and shout, it's not about your riffs and runs, it's not about how much money you can make, but it's about the advancement of the kingdom! And if we can ever get out of our own self, if we can ever stop making it about us, that's when we'll see people changed for real, that's when we'll see people delivered for real, that's when we'll see people saved for real. Your assignment is bigger than you!

I would be remised if I didn't tell you that before God can release us into his designed season for our lives, he first takes us through a process. The significance of this process is to first prepare us for our next level. Have you ever noticed that before God shifts you into a new season, your warfare is seemingly more intensified? And that is because adverse times are generally associated with elevation.

Adversity usually signifies that a shifting is about to take place.

Can I help somebody when I tell you that our adversity is not always God's way of punishing us, but rather it is sometimes God's way of developing necessary characteristics for a greater season?

David said it best when he declared that it was good for me that I was afflicted.

This further lets me know that all adversities are not bad adversities. I know we want to believe that every challenging situation is a direct attack of the enemy, and we start blaming the devil for all the hell we are experiencing.

But can I help somebody when I tell you that all adversities are not sent by the devil? Sometimes God has to shake up your situation in order to get us somewhere. Sometimes hell needs to break loose in your life. Sometimes it's good that people are talking about you. Every day can't be sunny. Every once in a while, you need some rain. Why? Because these things are producing something in you for where God is about to take you that only adversity can birth out! And a lot of times, we desire the season but omit the process. We desire God to take us higher but omit what comes along with the territory. But one thing about the process is that God will use your adversity as a catalyst to push you into destiny, but can you handle the process?

David now was anointed by Samuel to be a king. But instead of David who immediately took his reign, David went back to his original assignment which was tending to his father's sheep, in which further suggests to me that just because you are anointed does not make you ready. And can I tell you that we, the church, have let excitement push us outside of the timing and will of God for our lives?

That's why nowadays, we have so many people that are operating in the church with a lot of zeal but don't have any substance. They have a lot of zeal but no knowledge. They have a lot of zeal but no preparation. They have a lot of zeal but no endurance. They have zeal but no experience. And the problem nowadays is that we have too many people who want to operate but don't want to be taught, to sit down, and to be trained.

In the old church, the older saints would tell you before you try, do something, sit down, and *learn* yourself something because they understood that fulfilling purpose takes more than just excitement. It takes more than just eagerness, but they knew that you are going to need some foundation to build on.

As we place our attention back to the text, what's amazing for me is while David's brothers were positioning themselves to reign as Israel's next king, David was in the field working all the while. They were dressing up and feasting. David was in the field working while they were prorated in the presence of Samuel. David was in the field working! When it was evident God had rejected them, only then was David sought after.

What I love about it is David didn't have to politicize with anybody. David didn't have to tear somebody else down for a position. David didn't have to be a part of certain clicks, but when it was his time, they found him working!

And I come to tell somebody that your time is not determined by who you're associated with, it's not determined by how many connections you got but rather by your faithfulness to what God has assigned you over. The Bible says that if we humble ourselves under the mighty hand of God that he will exalt us in due season.

While David's brothers were indulging, David had his hand to the plow. God saw David's diligence over what father loved in which was a direct indication that he could be trusted with something greater! And when God trust you with what he loves, he can then entrust you with greater than where you are.

And can I help somebody when I tell you that some of us are still in the same position simply because God can't trust us yet. We are too busy seeking platforms and big names and not concerned about what God's heart has. Why don't you just touch somebody and ask the neighbor: Can God trust you?

What really blessed me about this portion of the text is that while David's brothers were at the table, the feast was prepared for David. They didn't know it yet, but they were just partakers of David's festivities. And God told me to tell the people of God that just because the people that look the part are at the table, doesn't mean there the guest of honor! They may have the connections, they may have the status, they may have the resources, but you have the oil of God.

God said you're about to go from seeking to being sought after. God is about to call you in!

ABOUT THE AUTHOR

T.Nicole, MBA is a native of Shreveport, Louisiana, where she holds an undergraduate degree in business management and holds a master's in business administration. T.Nicole has sustained a career in hotel management for the past six years as well as been active in ministry for the last seven years at the New Love Restoration Church under the direction of her pastor and her first lady, Lovelle and April Butler. T.Nicole is a firm believer in the great commission to go onto the highways and hedges and compel men. Her ultimate goal in life is to inspire, motivate, and help all crosses of life build on their relationship with God!

CPSIA information can be obtained
at www.ICGtesting.com
Printed in the USA
LVHW030334151019
634227LV00002B/674/P

9 781644 718919